Start Scrapbooking

*Dedicated to the
memory of my Mum,
Evelyn Scott, who gave
me so many precious
moments to scrapbook.*

Start Scrapbooking

Joy Aitman

SEARCH PRESS

First published in Great Britain 2005

Search Press Limited
Wellwood, North Farm Road,
Tunbridge Wells, Kent TN2 3DR

Text copyright © Joy Aitman 2005

Photographs by Charlotte de la Bédoyère, Search Press Studios
Photographs and design copyright © Search Press Ltd 2005

ISBN 1 84448 044 5

The Publishers and author can accept no responsibility for any
consequences arising from the information, advice or
instructions given in this publication.

Readers are permitted to reproduce any of the items/patterns
in this book for their personal use, or for the purposes of selling
for charity, free of charge and without the prior permission of
the Publishers. Any use of the items/patterns for commercial
purposes is not permitted without the prior permission of
the Publishers.

Suppliers
If you have difficulty in obtaining any of the materials and
equipment mentioned in this book, then please write to the
Publishers, at the address above, for a current list of stockists,
including firms who operate a mail-order service. This list also
details some of the fonts used in scrapbooking projects.

Publisher's note
All the step-by-step photographs in this book feature the
author, Joy Aitman, demonstrating scrapbooking. No
models have been used.

Maufactured by Universal Graphics Pte Ltd, Singapore
Printed in Malaysia by Times Offset (M) Sdn Bhd

Acknowledgements
I would like to thank:

*Mark, Rosie, Jake, Grace and Duncan for
their patience and for letting me take so
many photographs of them;*

Dad for his wise words;

Joanne for her encouragement;

*Vesutor for the Sandylion albums;
Kuretake for the pens;
Tonic for the trimmers and scissors;*

Sophie, Roz and Juan for all their help;

Lotti for her excellent photographs.

Contents

Introduction

My love of scrapbooking began five years ago. I have always been a keen photographer and dabbled in many crafts. Scrapbooking was the missing link: it brought the crafts and the photography together.

With four children, I take lots of photographs. I have recorded all the important events in their lives and of course all those little moments that do not seem so important at the time. They each have a scrapbook album which chronicles their life so far and they get lots of enjoyment from reading it themselves and showing it off to others.

Scrapbooking is also a fantastic way to keep a diary of the year. We scrapbook birthday parties, holidays, days out, school events and seasonal celebrations. I always try to have my camera with me, although photographs are not always necessary to create a layout.

The pages can be as simple or as complicated as you want them to be. It is a hobby you can do on your own or you can join others for a crop to swap ideas and show off layouts. It is also a hobby which spans the generations. Grandparents, parents and children can sit down together and create a scrapbook to pass on for the enjoyment of future generations.

I hope that you enjoy the projects in this book and that you will be searching out your old photographs and mementoes to create a scrapbook of your own. The book gives you the basic techniques and some ideas to get you started. As soon as you start sorting through your own photographs, you will be brimming over with ideas for your own layouts. Happy sorting and happy scrapping.

Materials

The materials for scrapbooking must be of a quality that will preserve your photographs and memorabilia. Materials used in the past such as sugar paper books, sticky tape, gum type glue and 'magnetic' albums with sticky strips were damaging to photographs.

Albums, card, paper, pens and adhesives must be acid free. Acid in paper or card causes the paper itself to deteriorate and also migrates into photographs, turning them yellow, faded and brittle. Acidic adhesives can literally eat away the emulsion from photographs. Paper should also be lignin free, since lignin causes the paper to brown and crumble.

Buy scrapbooking products from well-known scrapbooking companies and learn to look at labels. You should be looking for acid free, photo-safe or archival quality.

Granny and baby

In the bottom right-hand corner you can see where the acid adhesive has eaten away the emulsion from the photograph.

Two girls

This is a colour photograph from the 1970s that has changed colour because it was kept in an unsuitable album.

Nurses

Here the photographic emulsion has been eaten away at the edges and from behind, causing extensive damage to the image.

Basic equipment

You do not need too many pieces of equipment to scrapbook but there are some essentials.

A personal trimmer or **mini guillotine** makes cropping your photographs quicker and easier, eliminating wobbly edges caused by scissors. They are safe for children to use.

Scissors should be comfortable and suitable for the task. I use a small, sharp pair for cutting around lettering or small shapes, and a larger pair for general cutting.

It is important to choose the right **adhesive** for the job. Double-sided **photo stickers** or **tape**, which comes on a runner, are suitable for photographs. So is **repositionable tape**, which is useful for attaching items temporarily and becomes permanent if left. Never use a wet adhesive for photographs. **Glue dots** are essential for sticking down heavy embellishments. A **glue pen** is handy for small paper items such as punched shapes. **PVA glue** is a good, strong adhesive, useful for sticking down heavy embellishments.

Pens, used for journaling or decorating pages, should be acid free, waterproof and fade resistant. I have used calligraphy, fine point, double-ended and dotting pens.

Clockwise from bottom left: dotting, calligraphy, fine point and double-ended pens; a guillotine; paper scissors in two sizes; PVA glue with an applicator; an acid-free glue pen; a roll of glue dots, a repositionable tape runner and photo stickers.

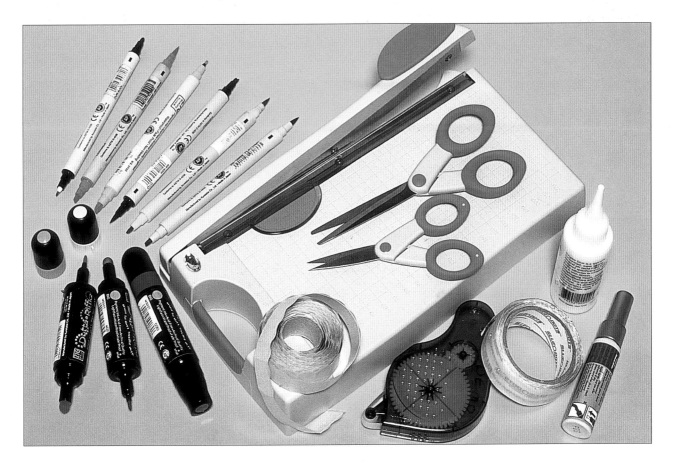

Albums

Albums should be acid free and sturdy. They come in a number of different styles and sizes but there are three basic types.

Ring-bound albums are very basic. They contain top-loading page protectors, which you fill with your finished layouts. They cannot be extended in any way.

Strap-bound albums are pages connected with flexible plastic straps. You work directly on to the pages and then cover them with slip-over protectors. They can be extended by threading more pages on to the strap.

Post-bound albums contain page protectors bound together with two to three screw posts. You put your finished layouts into the protectors back to back. They can be extended by using extension posts. They make it easiest to rearrange the order of your layouts and are my favourite.

The most popular size of album is 30.5 x 30.5cm (12 x 12in). Most cardstock and paper is cut to that size. Smaller albums are available in 21.6 x 28cm (8½ x 11in), 20.3 x 20.3cm (8 x 8in) and 15.2 x 15.2 (6 x 6in). These make good gift albums.

A selection of albums in different styles and sizes.

Paper

Cardstock is the mainstay of your album. It is cut in sizes to fit your album but usually comes in 30.5 x 30.5cm (12 x 12in). This is what you use as the background for your layouts, the mats for your photographs and for making embellishments. Make sure it is not too thick (160g is best). It must be acid and lignin free as it will be in direct contact with your photographs. A good scrapbooker will have a variety of colours on hand.

A good selection of **printed paper** will complement your cardstock. This is very much up to personal choice but do not let the patterns detract from your photographs. If the budget allows a few **specialist papers,** handmade, silk papers or vellums are always an attractive addition to a page.

Cardstock made to fit albums shown with a selection of papers and vellums used to decorate scrapbook pages.

Embellishments

I love bumpy pages and use a variety of embellishments on my layouts. However, do try and choose flattish objects to avoid tearing page protectors or damaging photographs on other layouts.

Wire is great for creating your own embellishments. It comes in a variety of different colours and thicknesses and can be easily shaped. It should be cut using **wire cutters**, not your scissors. I like to use it with **buttons** in all different themes or **beads**, especially seed beads and alphabet beads.

Paper punches provide a variety of shapes for your layouts. Punch out paper, card, cork and metal.

Fibres can be used to loop through tags or form borders. You can also thread a **needle** and stitch with fibres. They come in luscious colours and textures.

Tags can be all different shapes and types, from luggage tags to metal-rimmed circles. Use pre-made tags or create your own.

Fabric and **haberdashery** such as ribbons, twill tape and embroidery silks are becoming increasingly popular.

A **paper piercer** and **cork mat** will help you create holes for sewing.

Metal embellishments can give your pages a more masculine look. I love charms, washers and hinges.

Self-adhesive mesh comes in a variety of colours and can make great borders.

Coloured glue sticks and a **hot glue gun** can be used to create faux wax seals. Rub them with **gilt wax** to make them extra special.

Gesso creates a surface on embellishments which will hold chalks and paints.

Jigsaw pieces can be coloured with chalks to match your layout.

Paper punches, twill tape, fibres, a paper piercer and cork mat, needles, wire cutters, eyelets and snaps, beads and alphabet beads, charms and washers, wire, tags and envelopes, self-adhesive mesh, glue sticks with a hot glue gun and tile, white gesso, gilt paste and jigsaw pieces.

Other materials

A **30.5cm (12in) paper trimmer** is useful for cutting large pieces of cardstock. Every scrapbooker has a favourite. They come with a variety of cutting methods: sliding, rotary or guillotine blades.

A **craft knife** has a number of uses. I particularly like them for cutting out titles. It is good to try a few different ones to find one that is comfortable for you. Make sure it has a safety cover. You will need to use it with a **cutting mat.** Choose a mat with a grid on it as this will make cutting and measuring easier.

Rubber stamps can add decoration to a page, and letter stamps can be used for titles or journaling. The **inkpads** must contain permanent and acid free ink.

A **heating tool** can be applied to stamped images and embossing powder to create some interesting effects.

Decorating chalks can be used to add colour. They can also be used to age pieces of card or embellishments.

An **eyelet tool kit** is used to attach eyelets and snaps, which are eyelets without the central hole on the front. They both make wonderful embellishments as well as fixing other elements in place. The kit consists of a hammer, setting mat, hole punch with a variety of different sized holes, and a setter to open out the backs of the eyelets or snaps and hold them firm.

A heating tool, paper trimmer, alphabet rubber stamps, eyelet tool kit, craft knives, blades and cutting mat, rubber stamps, decorating chalks and inkpad.

Techniques

Cropping

Cropping is the term used for cutting your photographs. This is done if you are not happy with their composition or content. We do not always take perfect photographs, and cropping will remove the empty spaces, the people we did not want, or those stray items that creep in at the edges. However, it is important that you do not remove all the background from photographs, as you want to be able to set the scene and tell a story. Never cut polaroids as you will release chemicals which will leak out and spoil your pages. Heritage photographs should be treated with great respect as you are unlikely to have the negatives. Keep them whole to preserve historical detail. You can colour copy heritage photographs if there is something you would like to crop.

Look carefully at your photographs. Choose five to six for your layout. Determine what you will need to crop to focus on the theme of your layout. You can leave some photographs whole – do not get too carried away!

If you want to give cropped photographs a straight edge, use your mini guillotine to crop them. You can also use a template and scissors or a cutting system to cut them into other shapes such as circles or ovals.

Paula's wedding day
Wedding photographs look particularly good cropped into ovals.

Duncan goes exploring
This picture remains uncropped to emphasise the smallness and the adventurous nature of the boy.

A very windswept Rosie
Crop away all the background to make the subject fill the frame.

Not many of us can take the perfect photograph. By cropping them we can make them look better. We can remove excess background, unwanted people or objects, blurs or flashbacks.

These photographs are shown uncropped on the right, and cropped below.

Duncan rolls away

The excess space has been removed from the top and side of this photograph.

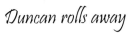

Washing Dad's car

The top has been taken off to remove the car from the girl's head. A small section has then been removed from the side to balance the shape of the photograph.

Helping Daddy

A section has been taken from the right-hand side to remove the toppled chair.

Matting

Matting is the process of putting photographs on a coloured cardstock mat. This can add definition to your photograph, enhance the colours and add interest to the page. Photographs can be matted in a number of different ways, but the simplest way is shown below.

1. Apply glue to the back of your photograph using repositionable tape as shown here. You can also use photo stickers.

2. Leave a small border. To help you to get the photograph straight, try to line up its edges with the machine-cut edges of the cardstock.

3. Cut round the image using scissors and leaving a border of backing card.

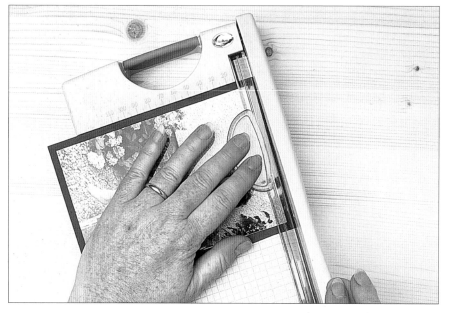

4. Use the guillotine to trim one side of the cardstock to match the borders on the other sides. Trim the remaining side to match and you are ready to position the matted photograph on your layout.

On the boardwalk

A photograph mat does not need to be a solid piece of card.

Grace

A torn mat can be very effective.

Kate and Wayne's wedding

A simple, classic mat is the most suitable for wedding photographs.

St. Ives

Have fun experimenting with different types of matting.

Choosing colour

Choosing the colours on your page is a very personal thing. We all have our favourite colour palettes; however, choosing the right colours is the key to a good page. Colour creates the mood and can enhance the photographs. New scrapbookers often find it difficult to choose and worry that they will make the wrong choice. Remember that the colours must ultimately please you and will reflect your personality. A colour wheel can be a useful addition to your tool bag as an aid to choosing combinations of colours.

When creating a layout there are two simple ways to choose your colours: firstly, being led by the colours in the photograph. By looking at the photographs you can often select colours that match or complement those that you can see. Do not choose more than four colours as this will confuse the eye. In the example I have selected two; the red from the jacket and the blue from the trim. I will use the tartan from the skirt as an embellishment.

Colour choice led by the photograph

Here the photograph itself has led the choice of cardstock colour and embellishments.

Blue for a boy

Traditional blue was chosen to complement the black and white baby photograph below, whereas Christmas themed colours work well in the page on the left.

Secondly by considering the theme of the layout; people tend to associate particular colours with events, celebrations, moods or seasons. A Christmas layout (below) could have red, green and gold; beach layouts blue and sand; baby layouts blue or pink. In the example shown right the photograph is black and white so I had no colour reference points. The baby is a boy, so I have chosen a very traditional blue for my cardstock, patterned paper and embellishments.

It is best to start with two colours, one for your background and one for your mat. Other colours can be added with embellishments. Lay the photograph on both colours and decide which way round looks best. A very light or dark photograph can be transformed by the colour you choose to mat it on. A dark photograph can be lifted with a light mat and a light photograph can be muted on a dark mat. The coloured mat will also define the edges of the photograph and make them stand out on the page. For some special photographs you may want to double or triple mat them.

Bounce

In this layout I have looked at the colours in the t-shirt and have been led by them. I matted the photograph on the lighter blue because the colours in the background of the photograph are quite dark. Although there is a lot of green in the photograph I felt that if I selected green cardstock as well, the whole layout would become dominated by green.

Layout

The first thing you need to decide is whether you are creating a single or double-page layout. This will influence how many photographs you use and how you arrange them. There is no correct number of photographs to put on a layout. It is not unusual to create a layout with a single photograph or capture an event with ten to twelve photographs. Be led by how many photographs you have taken – you may need to create an entire album for a special event! Choose a theme for your page; this will help you choose colours and embellishments.

Apart from your photographs, you will also need to think about the placement of a title, journaling and embellishments and arranging them to create a balanced layout.

There is usually a logical order to a series of photographs from an event. They make most sense if they are arranged chronologically. There may be one photograph that is a key focus, and that should be given predominance.

Sometimes a layout comes together very quickly, other times you feel as if you are solving a jigsaw puzzle. It is worth persevering to get it right, but remember, every layout does not have to be perfect.

Discover

This double-page layout has eight photographs on it but it does not look crowded. There is plenty of space separating each element. The shape and positioning of the photographs makes the two pages mirror images of each other, and this helps to balance the layout.

Brother and sister

This is a single-page layout and you can clearly see where I have divided the page vertically into thirds. The various elements are then positioned within their own third to create a balanced page.

Sleep

This is a single-page layout with three quite large photographs. I have created balance by dividing the page into thirds in both directions and placing the page elements at key points within this grid.

Journaling

Journaling is the documenting of facts or feelings on the page. It helps you to remember and to tell the story to others looking at your album whether in the past or the present. You can write as little or as much as you want to, but do write something. It is a good prompt to use the four Ws: who, what, when and where? This is useful historical documentation for future generations. You may also want to include quotations, poems or song lyrics.

There are different ways to journal and it is nice to incorporate a variety of methods in your album.

Handwriting

By writing on your page I feel that you leave a little bit of yourself on the layout, stamping your personality and style for others to enjoy. It does not matter if you do not like your own handwriting, nobody ever does!

Choose your pens from the wide selection that is available, making sure they are acid free. Fine liners, calligraphy pens and dot pens can be used on their own or together.

Practise what you are going to write so that you know how much space you will need. Use pencil lines as a guide, and erase them later.

Embellishing your title with flowers

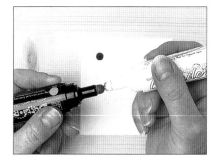

1. You can create flowers to decorate handwriting. Make a dot on scrap paper with a dark marker pen. Press the pink pen to the blender pen.

2. Touch the the dark dot with the blender pen.

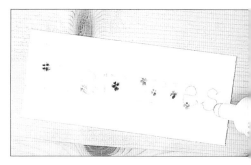

3. Do your handwriting in pencil. Press the blender pen down on the writing to make flower shapes.

4. Go over the pencilled writing with a black pen.

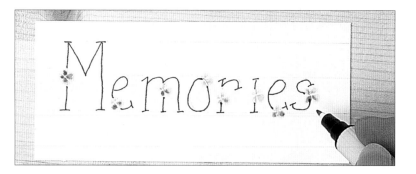

Layered writing

Build up layers with different shades of the same colour. Start with the lightest first. Experiment with different pens to achieve different effects. Scroll and brush pens are a lot of fun.

1. You can layer writing with brush pens. Write in pencil first, then go over it with the first colour.

2. Then go over it with a second pen in a different tone of the same colour.

Shadowed writing

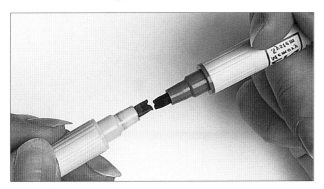

1. For another effect, press the scroll end of a pen against another colour.

2. Write with the first pen to create a shadowed effect.

Dot writing

Simple writing can be made more interesting with the addition of dots.

Using envelopes, pockets and mini-books

These are a different way to journal, so that your journaling does not have to be on display if you want to keep it personal. They are fun to create and they can be quite decorative. You can use pre-made items or make your own to match your layout.

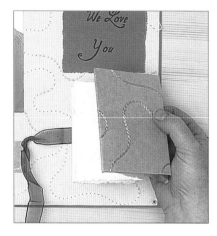

1. More personal things can be written in a concertina style 'book'.

2. This is then tied up with a ribbon.

Time layout
Write on tags placed in simple stitched pockets.

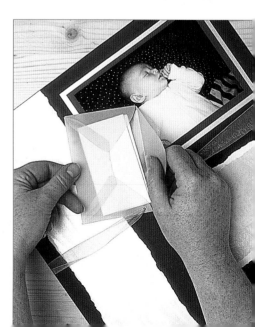

Baby layout
A letter can be tucked into a small vellum envelope.

Using alphabet stamps

Alphabet stamps are available in a number of different styles and sizes. Look for ones that suit your style of scrapbooking. Experiment with the effects that you can achieve by stamping on to different surfaces. Chalks can be used to create a more subtle, pastel effect. Stamp using a watermark pad and then dust with the chalks using a cotton wool ball. By combining different colours of chalk you can achieve very different looks.

1. Take some pieces from a cheap cardboard jigsaw. Paint over the pictures using white acrylic gesso or paint.

2. When the paint is dry, use a make-up applicator to apply coloured chalk.

3. Use a black inkpad and alphabet stamps to stamp the words you need on to the jigsaw pieces.

Pieces of me

Create your own embellishments and personalise them using alphabet stamps.

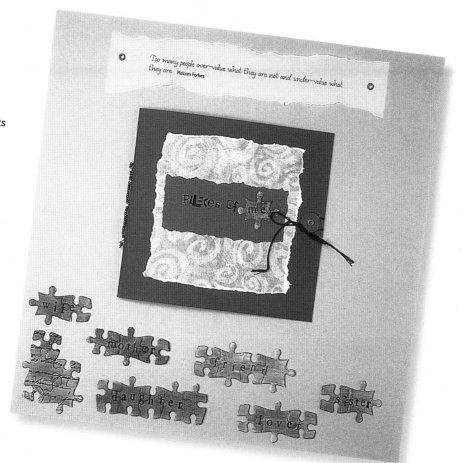

Printing

Journaling can be printed on to a variety of surfaces including tags, vellums, acetates (ink-jet), twill tape, ribbon and fabric.

1. Print out your text on standard A4 printer paper.

2. Apply repositionable adhesive tape to the back of the item you wish to print on.

3. Fix it over the text, making sure it is secure.

4. Run the paper back through the printer, overprinting on to the item. Then you can peel off the item and rub off the adhesive.

Tip

If you are printing on acetate or vellum, set your printer to the transparency setting.

January layout

Print on an ink-jet transparency to create a layered look. Experiment with different colours and fonts.

Daffodils layout

Print on to vellum and lay it over a photograph for a soft look.

Using alphabet beads, buttons and charms

This is a fun way of creating titles or highlighting particular words in your journaling. The beads and buttons can be stuck down individually or threaded on to wire to create words. The metal charms can be stuck or eyeleted on. Try different combinations of styles, colours and materials.

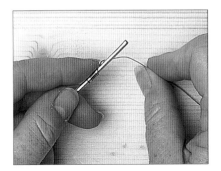

1. Take a length of 24 gauge wire and wind it round a small post to create a spiral at one end.

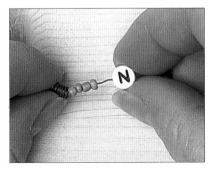

2. Thread your beads and alphabet beads on to the straight section of the wire.

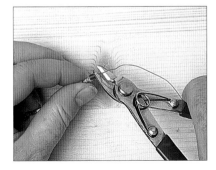

3. When you have finished threading on the beads, make another spiral at the end and trim the wire using wire cutters.

4. Press a glue dot on to the back of each alphabet bead and attach the beaded wire to your design.

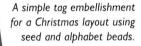

A simple tag embellishment for a Christmas layout using seed and alphabet beads.

Duncan

A title can be created using a combination of glass and alphabet beads.

Using eyelets

Eyelets can be functional or decorative on a page. They are metal, usually aluminium, and will not rust. They come in a variety of shapes, sizes and colours, but they are all set in the same way.

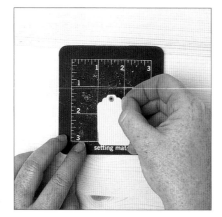

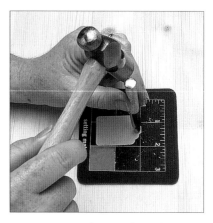

1. Mark on your card where you wish to make the hole for your eyelet. Select the size of the hole to match your eyelet. Place your card on a setting mat. Do not use your cutting mat as it will be damaged. Hold the punch upright with your fingers close to the paper. Strike the punch firmly with the hammer. You should be able to punch through one layer of card with one hit.

2. Put the neck of the eyelet through the hole.

3. Turn over the card so that the neck of the eyelet is facing up. Place the right sized setter head into the neck of the eyelet. Strike firmly with the hammer. The back of the eyelet will now flatten to look like a flower.

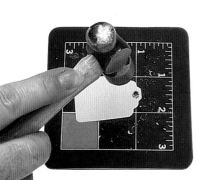

4. Remove the setter and hammer the eyelet once more to make sure it is flush to the paper.

The finished tag. Placing an eyelet in the hole makes it look more professional.

Using eyelets to attach four corners

When you attach a piece of card, paper or vellum by four corners it is important that you follow the correct order to prevent twisting.

1. Place a small strip of repositionable adhesive on the reverse of the item you want to eyelet. Mark where you are going to make the holes.

2. Place on to the layout and punch the first hole in the top left-hand corner. Set the eyelet. Punch the hole in the top right-hand corner and set the eyelet. If you are using vellum, remove the repositionable adhesive. You can now punch and set the other two holes.

Using eyelets for decoration

Eyelets can be used on their own to create simple embellishments or combined with other elements.

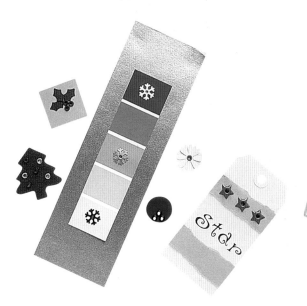

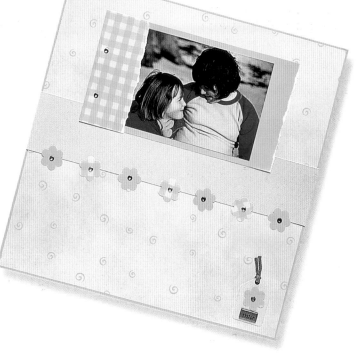

29

Embellishments

Embellishments can make your page look extra special. They can be as simple or as complicated as you wish. Do take care not to over-embellish your page: remember your photographs are the most important element on the page.

Wire, button and bead border

Wire is one of my favourite embellishments. It is very versatile and easy to use. It can be curled, twisted and shaped. It can be used for threading buttons and beads on and it comes in a variety of colours and thicknesses. The higher the gauge, the finer the wire.

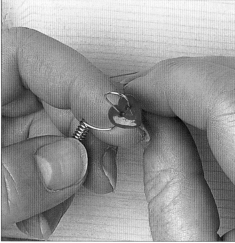

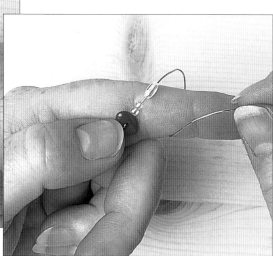

1. Cut the wire double the length of the border. Thread the wire through the holes on the first button as if you are making a stitch. Pull tight to secure the button. Leave a 6cm (2³⁄₈in) tail.

2. Make a loop in the wire and thread on some beads and the second button. Repeat until your border is long enough. Leave a 6cm (2³⁄₈in) tail.

The finished border. I have curled the tails at both ends round a skewer to create a spring shape. I have then stuck the border on to the cardstock by attaching glue dots to the buttons.

Using buttons with shanks

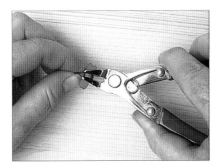

1. Cut the shank off the button with a pair of wire cutters. Cut as close to the base of the button as possible.

2. Stick the button on with a glue dot. This means you will not have to wait for the glue to dry.

Sunflower

Three sunflower buttons add colour to the layout.

Fibres and threads – stitching on the page

The secret to stitching on your page is to make the holes first using a template. This is particularly important if you are stitching a word.

1. Print out your word in the correct size and font. Attach to your layout with repositionable adhesive. Place the card on a mat – an old mouse mat would do, or a cork tile. Pierce holes with a paper piercer.

2. Remove the template and stitch with stranded embroidery thread in back stitch. Take care not to pull too tightly to avoid tearing the card.

The finished tag. I have added a 'sewn-on' patch and a ribbon in the same colour as the stitching.

31

Seaside Pictures

Most people have seaside pictures in their collections and like to scrapbook them to remember their holidays. These are always a good set of photographs to get you started in scrapbooking as they have a very definite theme. This makes choosing colours, patterned papers and embellishments much easier. My photographs are of an exotic trip to Indonesia.

You will need

Three photographs
30.5 x 30.5cm (12 x12in)
cardstock: one sheet Pool blue;
two sheets Cocoa brown
30.5 x 30.5cm (12 x12in)
patterned paper: Antique maps
Repositionable tape
Gilt wax
Luggage tag
Blue hot glue stick
Mini hot glue gun
Blue fibres
Craft glue dots
Ceramic tile
Shell rubber stamp
Craft knife and cutting mat
Scissors

1. Tear the antique map paper to create a 7–8cm (2¾–3¼in) wide strip. Tear the paper towards you to expose the white layer.

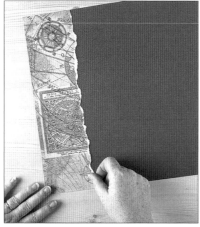

2. Use repositionable tape to stick the torn strip to the left-hand side of the brown card.

3. Place the photograph on the blue card and use scissors to cut round it, leaving an even border as shown.

4. Tear the edges of the blue backing rectangle towards you.

5. Mat all the photographs in the same way and place two on the backing sheet of the left-hand page using repositionable tape.

6. Tear antique map paper to trim the right-hand side of the right-hand page and place the third photograph as shown.

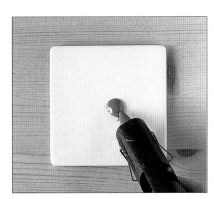

7. Heat the hot glue gun with the blue glue stick inside. Squeeze a circle of glue approximately 3cm (1¼in) in diameter on to your tile.

8. Press the rubber stamp in to the glue and leave it to set. Remove the stamp.

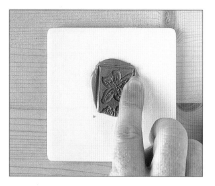 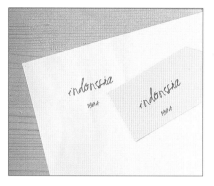 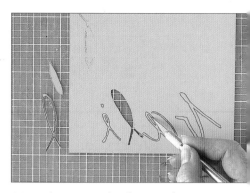

9. Rub a little gilt wax on to the 'seal' with your fingertip. A little goes a long way.

10. Print the luggage label with the place name and date, using the method shown on page 26.

11. Select an italic font and outline style and type your title. Use the draw program to flip the image vertically so that it is reversed, and print it on to blue cardstock. Cut it out with a craft knife or small scissors. The black outline will not show as it will be on the reverse.

Seaside Pictures

I particularly liked the antique map paper which gave the look of a more exotic destination. I chose a dark brown background to complement the turquoise blue of the sea and the sky in the photographs.

12. Assemble the two scrapbook pages and stick down the various elements. Use glue dots to attach the wax seal, glue pen for the cut-out lettering and repositionable tape for the luggage label.

St. Ives

Cornwall
February 2004

Duncan had a lovely time
playing on the beach. He
was happy to sit on his
own building castles.

[ad·ven´·ture]

sun   sea   sand

The beach in winter

The colours and embellishments chosen reflect the cold and ruggedness of a winter beach.

sand

sticks

castle

Happy

Sunset on the shore

The warmth of the sunset is captured with
the use of brightly coloured transparencies
and metallic slide mounts.

Lazy days

St. Ives
2004

School Picture

We all have pictures of either ourselves as children, our own children or our grandchildren posing for their yearly school portrait photograph. It is a challenge to create a different layout for each photograph. In this layout I have attempted the look of a cork notice board decorated with a collection of school essentials.

1. Use a paper trimmer or mini guillotine to trim the cork, taking 6mm (1/4in) from the top and one side.

3. Use alphabet stamps and an inkpad to stamp the small brown envelope with the words 'lunch money'.

2. Use glue dots to attach the cork centrally on the backing card. Mat the photograph on card of the same colour, leaving a 5mm ($^3/_{16}$ in) border all the way round, and place the matted photograph as shown on the cork 'notice board'.

4. Print out the child's name on an ordinary sheet of A4 paper. Position the length of twill tape over the lettering and print the name on the tape as shown on page 26.

5. Write on the library card as shown.

6. Fix the snaps to each end of the name tag, following the same method as for eyelets shown on page 28.

7. Write on the scrap of notepaper and attach a snap to one corner. Tear off the corner of a letter from school which shows the school badge. Assemble the page as shown and stick everything down using repositionable tape or photo stickers.

Jake's year at school

This layout can be added to throughout the year, with tickets for the nativity play, a school council badge, or any other reminders – just like your notice board at home.

Nursery days

Children start school younger and younger. Don't forget to scrapbook nursery days as well.
Use an inspirational quotation for your title.

St. Aiden's College

Durham

1984

Graduation

A simple graduation layout using pre-made embellishments and a hand-cut title as described on page 34.

Wedding Picture

We all take photographs, or have our photograph taken, at weddings. It is a special day and we want our layouts to look special too. I always think that wedding pages should be simple and clean cut so that the main focal point is the photograph.

Choose colours that match the wedding dress or the bridesmaids' dresses and if you are doing a whole album, repeat these on each page to tie all the pages together. Remember to include invitations, order of service sheets, menus, confetti and other mementoes of the day.

1. Tear out three 40mm (1½in) diameter circles, three 35mm (1⅜in) diameter circles and three 30mm (1¼in) diameter circles in red card. Tear three leaf shapes approximately 30mm long from green card.

2. Crumple up all of your circles and leaves and then flatten them out. This gives the flowers a more three-dimensional look. Moisten your thumb and forefinger and use them to roll up the edges of the flowers, again to add dimension.

3. Layer the three sizes of circles to form three flowers and use the eyelet tool kit to secure a pewter eyelet in the centre of each one as shown on page 28.

4. Print your chosen quotation on twill tape as described on page 26. Mat the photograph and fix it on the page with repositionable tape or photo stickers. Attach the twill tape using double-sided tape.

5. Use glue dots to attach the flowers and leaves.

Grow old with me ... the best is yet to come

Red roses were the predominant theme of this page and the rest of the album.

Monica & Joseph

September 12th

1959

Salisbury

Rhodesia

Monica and Joseph

Older style or heritage wedding photographs look best with more subtle colours and appropriate embellishments such as ribbons and charms.

Index